MEMORABLE

ROASTS

TRADITIONAL FARE

A collection of mouthwatering roasts from classics such as Roast Beef with Horseradish Sauce and Traditional Roast Chicken to deliciously different newcomers. Try Indian-Style Lamb or Standing Rib Roast with Pâté. All are sure to delight family and friends.

MURDOCH BOOKS

Sydney • London • Vancouver

BEEF AND VEAL

Traditional Roast Beef with Gravy

*T*he tradition of a beef or veal roast seems to signify a special meal. Few can resist the impressive sight of these traditional roasts at the dinner table awaiting carving. Their richly coloured crusts and tender juicy meat are perennial favourites. Beef and veal roasts combine beautifully with the full-bodied flavours of red wine, gravy, garlic, mustard and pungent horseradish to make a truly mouth-watering treat.

Suitable cuts for roasting include Scotch fillet or fillet, rump, rib roast, yearling bolar blade, topside and fresh silverside. Veal roasts include the leg, loin rack and shoulder.

COOKING TIMES

To calculate cooking time, always weigh after trimming excess fat from the meat.
Guidelines for Roasting Beef and Veal
Rare: 20–25 minutes per 500 g
Medium: 25–30 minutes per 500 g
Well done: 30–35 minutes per 500 g
To determine doneness, if using a meat thermometer, insert it into the thickest part of flesh away from fat or bone for accurate readings. The internal temperature should be 60° for rare meat, 70° for medium, and 75° for well done.
The 'pinch' test is also a good way to test for doneness. Give the centre of the meat a quick pinch — the more yielding it is the rarer the meat will be.

Traditional Roast Beef with Gravy

Preparation time:
 10 minutes
Cooking time: 1½ hours
Serves 6

2.5 kg piece roasting
 beef, trimmed of
 excess fat
freshly ground black
 pepper
1 clove garlic, crushed
Gravy
2 teaspoons plain flour
2 tablespoons red wine
1¼ cups beef stock
freshly ground black
 pepper

1 Rub outside of meat with pepper and garlic. Place on a rack in a baking dish.

2 Bake in a moderate oven (180°), allowing 25 minutes per 500 g for medium rare, or a little longer if well done meat is required. Cover loosely with foil. Stand for 15 minutes before carving.
3 To prepare Gravy: drain off all except 1 tablespoon of fat from baking dish. Place dish over a low heat. Add flour. Stir well to incorporate all the sediment. Cook, stirring constantly, over medium heat until well browned, taking care not to burn.
4 Combine wine and stock. Gradually stir into flour mixture. Heat, stirring constantly, until gravy boils and thickens. Cook for 3 minutes. Season.
5 Serve Roast Beef with gravy, baked vegetables, Yorkshire Pudding, carrots and broccoli or other vegetables.

HINT
If serving Roast Beef with Yorkshire Puddings you will need to keep the beef in a warm spot while the oven is hot for baking the puddings. If serving roast potatoes, crisp them in the hot oven while baking the puddings.

HOW TO CARVE A RIB ROAST

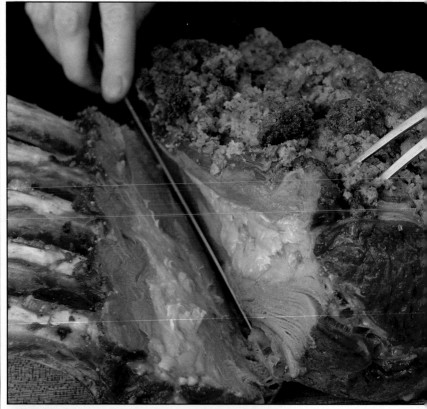

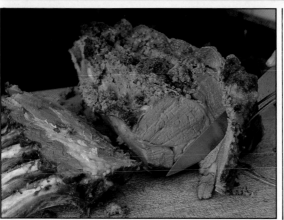

1 Remove upper spinal bones. Try not to pierce the meat. Steady meat with the back of a carving fork. Separate meat from bone by cutting horizontally along contours of rib.
2 Slice the beef vertically. Each slice will fall free as you cut.

Standing Rib Roast with Pâté

Preparation time:
30 minutes
Cooking time: 1¾ hours
Serves 8

1 rasher rindless bacon,
  chopped
1 small onion, finely
  chopped
125 g mushrooms, finely
  chopped
125 g prepared
  peppercorn pâté
½ cup dry breadcrumbs
2 tablespoons chopped
  fresh parsley
¼ teaspoon dried mixed
  herbs
freshly ground black
  pepper to taste
1 egg, lightly beaten

3 kg standing rib roast
  (see note)

1 Place bacon in a dry frying pan. Heat gently until beginning to soften. Add onion and mushrooms. Cook, stirring, for about 3 minutes. Transfer to a bowl. Mix in pâté, breadcrumbs, parsley, herbs, pepper and egg.
2 Cut a slit in meat between rib bones and outer layer of fat at the narrow end. Remove any excess fat.
3 Fill cavity with pâté mixture. Replace flap. Secure with a skewer if necessary.
4 Place meat in a baking dish fat side up (the bones form a natural rack). Bake in a very hot oven (220°) for 15 minutes. Reduce to moderate (180°). Continue to bake for a further 1½ hours or until done to taste.
5 Allow to rest for 15 minutes before carving. Serve with gravy, horseradish, roast potatoes and vegetables.

Note: Ask your butcher to help prepare your roast by sawing through the upper spinal bones, so that they will be easy to remove before carving (see How to Carve a Rib Roast). Calculate cooking time at 20 minutes per 500 g. This will achieve a roast which is well done on the outside and rare on the inside.

Standing Rib Roast with Pâté

5

Beef with Blue Cheese in Pastry

Preparation time:
  45 minutes
Cooking time:
  30 minutes
Serves 8

1 *bunch spinach or*
  500 g frozen spinach
60 *g butter or margarine*
1.5 *kg piece topside,*
  trimmed
2 *sheets frozen puff*
  pastry, thawed
200 *g blue vein cheese,*
  softened
1 *sheet puff pastry extra*
  (optional)
1 *egg, lightly beaten*

1 To prepare spinach: remove stalk from leaves by cutting along both sides of stalk through centre of each leaf. Wash leaves well. If using frozen spinach, allow to thaw. Squeeze out excess water before placing on pastry.
2 Drop leaves into boiling water. Cook for 30 seconds or until leaves are just softened. Drain. Refresh in cold water. Pat dry with paper towel. Set aside.
3 Heat butter in a large pan. Add meat. Brown on all sides to seal in juices. Cool. Retain pan juices.
4 Place pastry on a flat surface. Overlap edges by 1 cm. Press together well. Arrange spinach over pastry leaving a 5 cm border.
5 Spread or crumble cheese over spinach. Place beef in centre of pastry. Fold in narrow ends. Fold remaining pastry over to enclose beef. Turn seam to underside. Decorate with extra pastry if desired. Brush with egg.
6 Place on a lightly greased baking tray. Bake in a hot oven (200°) for 25–30 minutes or until pastry is golden. Rest, covered with foil, for 10 minutes before slicing. Serve with gravy and vegetables.

HINT
Pieces of meat are often 'seared' before roasting by browning quickly in hot butter or oil to seal in juices and to give a tender result.

Beef with Blue Cheese in Pastry

Peppered Beef Fillet with Béarnaise Sauce

Peppered Beef Fillet with Béarnaise Sauce

Preparation time:
45 minutes
Cooking time:
30 minutes
Serves 6

1 kg beef eye fillet
1 tablespoon oil
2 cloves garlic, crushed
1 tablespoon crushed
   black peppercorns
2 teaspoons crushed
   coriander seeds
Béarnaise Sauce
125 g butter
3 shallots, chopped
½ cup dry white wine
2 tablespoons tarragon
   vinegar
1 tablespoon fresh
   tarragon
4 egg yolks
1 tablespoon lemon juice

1 Trim fillet, removing any fat. Tie up with string to keep good shape. Brush with oil and garlic. Roll fillet in combined peppercorns and coriander seeds.
2 Place fillet on a rack in baking tray. Bake in a hot oven for 10 minutes. Reduce heat to moderate (180°). Cook for a further 20 minutes for medium rare or until done to taste. Stand, keeping warm, for 10–15 minutes.
3 To prepare Béarnaise Sauce: melt butter in a small saucepan. Continue heating until milky parts have separated off. Do not stir. Skim off milky sediment with a spoon. Set clear butter aside.
4 Place shallots, wine, vinegar and tarragon in a small saucepan. Cook rapidly until only 2 tablespoons of the liquid is left. Set aside.
5 Place egg yolks in food processor or blender. Process for 10 seconds. Add lemon juice. Process for 5 seconds. Slowly pour the melted butter in through the chute while the motor is running. Add seasonings and strained shallot mixture. Process for a few seconds. Serve peppered beef fillet warm with Béarnaise sauce.

HINT

The easiest way to test if a roast is done is by feel. Give the centre of the meat a quick pinch — the more yielding it is, the rarer the meat will be.

Loin of Veal with Peppercorn Sauce

Preparation time:
  30 minutes
Cooking time: 1½ hours
Serves 6

2 kg loin of veal, boned
2 tablespoons Dijon
  mustard
freshly ground pepper
1 tablespoon oil
15 g butter
1 cup dry white wine
bouquet garni
2 tablespoons brandy
¼ cup cream
1 tablespoon canned
  green peppercorns,
  drained

1 Place veal, fat side down, on a flat surface. Spread with 1 tablespoon of mustard and sprinkle with pepper.
2 Roll up veal, shaping neatly and tie securely with string. Spread fat layer of loin with remaining mustard.
3 Heat oil and butter in pan. Add veal. Cook slowly, turning to brown all sides. Transfer veal to roasting pan. Add wine and bouquet garni. Cover pan with foil.
4 Bake in a moderate oven (180°) basting frequently until veal is tender, about 1½ hours. Transfer veal to serving platter, remove string, cover and keep warm.

5 Strain cooking liquid into small pan. Discard bouquet garni. Skim off excess fat. Bring to the boil, reduce heat and simmer uncovered until reduced and thickened. Stir in brandy, cream and crushed green peppercorns. Do not boil.
6 Serve loin of veal thinly sliced with sauce.

Herbed Roast Beef with Sauce Bordelaise

Preparation time:
  30 minutes
Cooking time: 1½ hours
Serves 6

2.5 kg piece roasting
  beef, trimmed of
  excess fat
freshly ground black
  pepper
1 teaspoon ground
  thyme
1 teaspoon ground
  oregano
1 clove garlic, peeled
Sauce Bordelaise
1¼ cups beef stock
1 cup dry red wine
¼ cup tomato paste
30 g butter
2 bay leaves
2 teaspoons plain flour

1 Rub outside of meat with plenty of black pepper, ground thyme, oregano and garlic

clove. Place on a rack in a roasting pan.
2 Roast in a moderate oven (180°), allowing 25 minutes per 500 g for medium rare or a little longer if well done meat is required. Cover loosely with foil. Stand meat for 15–20 minutes before carving.
3 To prepare Sauce Bordelaise: combine stock, wine, tomato paste, butter and bay leaves in pan. Bring to boil. Reduce heat and simmer uncovered until reduced by half. Remove bay leaves.
4 Drain off all but 1 tablespoon of fat from roasting pan. Place pan over a medium heat, sprinkle in flour and stir well to incorporate all the sediment. Stir constantly until well browned. Gradually stir in stock and wine reduction. Stir constantly until sauce boils and thickens. Serve with herbed beef.

HINT
Roast meats all benefit from a short rest in a warm place before carving, keeping the juices within the meat and making it easier to carve.

Herbed Roast Beef with Sauce Bordelaise

Rack of Veal with Herbed Crust

Preparation time:
  30 minutes
Cooking time: 1–1½
  hours
Serves 6

1.5 kg rack of veal
  (6 cutlets)
1 cup fresh breadcrumbs
½ cup packaged dry
  breadcrumbs
1 tablespoon finely
  chopped parsley
1 tablespoon finely
  chopped basil
2 egg whites, lightly
  beaten
2 cloves garlic, crushed
1 tablespoon oil
30 g butter, melted
Lemon Sauce
¼ cup dry white wine
¼ cup water
2 tablespoons lemon
  juice
1 teaspoon sugar
90 g butter, cubed
2 teaspoons finely
  chopped parsley

1 Trim any excess fat
from veal. Combine
fresh and dry bread-
crumbs, parsley and
basil. Add combined egg
whites, garlic, oil and
butter. Mix well. Add a
little water if mixture is
too dry.
2 Press mixture firmly
over fatty side of rack.
Place rack, crust side up,
in a baking dish. Roast
in a moderately slow

oven (160°) for 1–1½
hours.
3 Allow meat to stand in
a warm place for 10–15
minutes before slicing.
Drain off all except 2
tablespoons of juice in
baking dish.
4 To prepare Lemon
Sauce: heat baking dish
on top of stove. Add
wine, water, lemon juice
and sugar. Bring to the
boil, reduce heat.
Simmer uncovered until
reduced to half a cup of
liquid.
5 Whisk in butter one
cube at a time. Add
parsley. Serve lemon
sauce over each veal
cutlet.

Note: Ask your butcher
to cut through bones for
ease of slicing.

HINT
Veal is a delicate kind
of meat and needs
only a moderate to
moderately slow oven
temperature. Leaner
cuts of veal such as
rump or loin need
extra fat to keep them
moist; use fresh pork
fat or baste with a
mixture of oil and
butter.

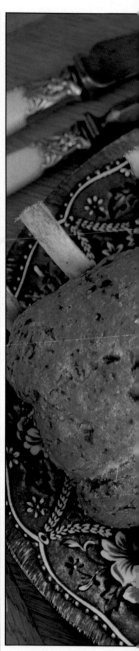

Rack of Veal with Herbed Crust

LAMB

Roast Lamb with Orange and Rosemary Stuffing, Wine Gravy, Onions in Cream and Broccoli with Browned Nut Butter Sauce

*S*pring is the time to enjoy tender succulent lamb; we boast some of the best in the world. Our recipes reflect the versatility of this meat by incorporating flavours from other lands to complement its distinctive taste.

The flavour of lamb roast is enhanced by the addition of garlic, rosemary, oregano, mint and lemon.

Suitable cuts for roasting include leg, shoulder, rib loin, racks of lamb and crown roast, breast and shanks.

Roast Lamb with Orange and Rosemary Stuffing

Preparation time:
 50 minutes
Cooking time: 1½ hours
Serves 6

2 kg leg of lamb, boned
1 cup fresh breadcrumbs
2 tablespoons finely
 chopped rosemary
2 tablespoons coarsely
 chopped pecans
1 tablespoon orange
 marmalade
2 teaspoons grated
 orange rind
2 tablespoons orange
 juice
1 tablespoon orange
 marmalade, extra
½ cup dry white wine
1 teaspoon grated
 orange rind, extra
2 tablespoons orange
 marmalade, extra

1 Trim excess fat from lamb; open out to a flat surface. Combine breadcrumbs, rosemary and pecans. Add combined marmalade, orange rind and juice. Mix lightly, adding extra orange juice if necessary to bind.
2 Press stuffing into cavity, roll up meat and tie securely at intervals with string. Place lamb in baking dish and brush with extra marmalade. Bake uncovered in a hot oven (220°) for 10–15 minutes, reduce heat to moderate (180°) and continue baking until tender and cooked as desired, about 1–1½ hours. Cover lamb with foil if it is browning too quickly. Stand, keeping warm, for 10–15 minutes before carving.
3 Place baking dish over a low heat. Add wine and stir well to incorporate any sediment. Bring to the boil, reduce heat and simmer until reduced to a thin sauce. Stir in extra orange rind and extra marmalade.
4 Remove string from lamb. Slice thinly. Spoon sauce over lamb to serve.

Note: Ask your butcher to bone the leg for you.

Roast Shoulder of Lamb with Mustard and Redcurrant Glaze

Preparation time:
 20 minutes
Cooking time: 1½ hours
Serves 6

2 kg shoulder of lamb
2 tablespoons Dijon
 mustard
¼ cup redcurrant jelly
1 clove garlic, crushed
2 teaspoons oil
2 teaspoons soy sauce

1 Trim excess fat from lamb. Combine mustard, jelly, garlic, oil and soy sauce. Brush glaze over lamb.
2 Place lamb on a rack over a baking dish. Add about ½ cup water to baking dish. Bake in a moderate oven (180°) basting frequently with pan juice for 1½ hours or until done as desired. Stand, keeping warm, for 10–15 minutes.
3 Serve glazed lamb with gravy.

Indian-Style Lamb

Preparation time: 40
  minutes plus overnight
  marinating time.
Cooking time: 1¾ hours
Serves 6

2 kg leg of lamb,
    trimmed of all fat
Marinade
⅓ cup almonds
2 medium onions,
    chopped
6 to 8 cloves garlic,
    peeled
5 cm piece ginger, peeled
4 teaspoons chopped
    chilli or 4 fresh
    chillies, chopped
1 x 500 g carton yoghurt
2 tablespoons lemon
    juice
¼ cup vegetable oil
½ teaspoon each ground
    coriander, cumin,
    cayenne pepper and
    garam masala
freshly ground black
    pepper

1 Make deep slashes in
leg of lamb with a small,
sharp knife. Place leg in
a baking dish. Set aside.
2 To prepare Marinade:
place almonds, onions,
garlic, ginger, chilli and
3 tablespoons yoghurt in
a food processor or
blender. Process until a
paste is formed. Paste
will be thick.
3 Transfer to a bowl.
Stir in remaining
ingredients. Spoon
marinade over lamb,
pushing some into
slashes in meat.
4 Turn leg over to ensure
that entire leg is covered
thickly with marinade.
Cover with plastic wrap.
Marinate in refrigerator
for at least 24 hours,
turning occasionally.
5 Allow meat to return
to room temperature
before baking. Remove
plastic wrap. Cover with
lid or foil. Bake in a
moderate oven (180°)
for 1¼ hours.
6 Uncover. Bake for a
further 20–30 minutes,
basting occasionally.
Stand meat to rest for 15
minutes before carving.
7 Remove any fat from
top of marinade in
baking dish. Serve
remaining marinade
with meat. If desired,
garnish meat with whole
toasted almonds and
sultanas.

Note: Roast lamb in a
glass rather than a metal
ovenproof dish so as not
to affect the flavour of
the sauce.

HINT
Baste is the culinary
term used for
spooning fat or liquid
over food during
cooking to prevent
food drying out.

Indian-Style Lamb

Rack of Lamb with Tropical Seasoning

Rack of Lamb with Tropical Seasoning

Preparation time:
50 minutes
Cooking time: 1 hour
Serves 4

racks of lamb, each
  with 6 cutlets
½ cup mint jelly
2 tablespoons pineapple
  juice

Tropical Seasoning
30 g butter
1 cup fresh breadcrumbs
1 cup crushed pineapple
1/4 cup pineapple juice
2 tablespoons finely
  chopped mint
1 teaspoon grated fresh
  ginger

Redcurrant Mint Sauce
1 tablespoon redcurrant
  jelly
1 tablespoon hot water
2 tablespoons red wine
  vinegar
2 tablespoons finely
  chopped mint

Trim excess fat from
lamb. Combine mint
jelly and pineapple
juice. Place racks fat
side up in baking dish.
Brush with mint jelly
mixture. Bake in a
moderate oven (180°)
for 3/4–1 hour or until
done as desired. Brush
with remaining glaze.
Cover and stand for
10–15 minutes before
slicing. Keep warm.
To prepare Tropical
Seasoning: heat butter in
pan. Add breadcrumbs.
Cook, stirring, until
golden. Stir in pineapple,
juice, mint and ginger.
Place in a heatproof dish,
cover and bake in a
moderate oven (180°)
for 15 minutes. Uncover
dish and bake for
15 minutes further or
until golden.
3 To prepare Redcurrant
Mint Sauce: combine all
ingredients in a small
pan. Cook, stirring, until
warm. Serve sliced racks
with Tropical Seasoning
and sauce.

Note: Ask your butcher
to cut through the bones
for ease of slicing.

Crusty Leg of Lamb

Preparation time:
  30 minutes
Cooking time: 1½ hours
Serves 6

2 kg leg of lamb
1 egg yolk, lightly beaten
60 g butter, melted
1 cup cornflake crumbs
1 tablespoon sesame
  seeds
½ teaspoon mixed herbs
1 small onion, sliced
½ cup water

1 Trim excess fat from
lamb. Brush top of
surface with a little egg
yolk.
2 Combine butter,
cornflake crumbs,
sesame seeds, mixed
herbs and half remaining
egg yolk. Press mixture
firmly over top of lamb.
Break onion slices into
rings and arrange in a
pattern over the crumb
surface, pressing with
the palm of your hand.
Brush onion rings with
rest of egg yolk.
3 Place lamb on a rack in
a baking dish. Add water
to baking dish. Cook in
a moderate oven (180°)
for about 1½ hours or
until cooked as desired.
When the crust becomes
golden and crisp, cover
with foil for the rest of
the cooking time. Add
more water to baking
dish when necessary.
4 Serve lamb with a mint
sauce and vegetables.

HINT

Roast meats on a rack
or trivet over a
baking dish. This will
avoid a fatty tasting
joint as excess fat
drips off to bottom of
baking dish. Add
about ½ cup water to
baking dish. This
prevents the fat
burning and keeps
joint moist. Replenish
when necessary.

Rack of Lamb with Chive Crust

Preparation time:
  30 minutes
Cooking time: 1 hour
Serves 4

½ cup dry breadcrumbs
2 teaspoons chopped
    fresh chives
2 teaspoons chopped
    mint
1 clove garlic, crushed
1 tablespoon lemon juice
1 teaspoon lemon rind
2 racks of lamb, each
    with 6 cutlets,
    trimmed
60 g butter or
    margarine, melted
Sauce
¼ cup white wine
¼ cup water
1 teaspoon brown sugar
1 tablespoon lemon juice
100 g butter, cubed
1 tablespoon mint jelly

1 Combine first six
ingredients in a small
bowl. A little water may
be required if mixture is
too dry.
2 Press mixture firmly
over fatty side of racks.
Drizzle butter over crust.
3 Place lamb racks,
crust side up, in a
baking dish. Bake in a
moderate oven (180°)
for ¾–1 hour.
4 Allow meat to rest
for 15 minutes before
slicing. Drain off all
except 2 tablespoons of
juice in pan.

5 To prepare Sauce:
place roasting pan on
top of stove and stir
wine and water into
juices. Bring to boil,
sitrring well. Boil until
reduced by half.
6 Stir in sugar and
lemon juice. Whisk in
butter one cube at a
time. Blend in mint jelly.

Note: Ask your butcher
to cut through the
bones for easy slicing.

HINT

Technically, lamb is a
young sheep no more
than a year old; at
two years it becomes
mutton. There is a
tendency to refer to
all meat of the sheep
as lamb. Both lamb
and mutton are
equally delicious,
lamb being very
tender and mutton
with a richer flavour
but requiring longer,
slower cooking.

HINT

Spring is the prime
time for tender young
lamb. Enjoy this
succulent favourite
while in season.

Rack of Lamb with Chive Crust

Roast Leg of Lamb with Redcurrant Sauce

Preparation time:
  30 minutes
Cooking time: 2 hours
Serves 6

2 leeks, sliced
¼ cup sultanas
¼ cup packaged stuffing
  mix
2 tablespoons pine nuts
1 tablespoon tomato
  sauce
1 egg, beaten
2 kg leg of lamb, boned
freshly ground black
  pepper to taste
¼ cup water
½ cup chicken stock
1 tablespoon brandy
1 tablespoon redcurrant
  jelly
1 tablespoon cornflour

1 Combine leeks, sultanas, stuffing mix, pine nuts, tomato sauce and egg. Mix well. Push mixture into opening in leg. Join opening with skewers and secure with string if necessary.
2 Slash fat on top side of leg with a sharp knife in a criss-cross pattern. Rub with pepper. Place meat fat side up on a rack in a baking dish. Bake in a moderate oven (180°) for 40 minutes.
3 Pour water into dish. Return to oven for a further 1½ hours or until meat is cooked as desired.
4 Stand lamb, keeping warm. Strain cooking liquid into a bowl. Return to baking dish with stock, brandy and jelly.
5 Blend cornflour with a little of the liquid to form a smooth paste. Stir into sauce. Heat, stirring constantly, until sauce boils and thickens. Reduce heat and simmer for 3 minutes. Serve roast with sauce and vegetables of choice.

Note: Ask your butcher to 'tunnel bone' the leg for you.

HINT
There is a variety of packet stuffings on the market. You can vary the flavour by adding other ingredients such as fresh herbs, spice and citrus rind.

Roast Leg of Lamb with Garlic and Rosemary

Preparation time:
  20 minutes
Cooking time: 1½ hours
Serves 6–10

2 kg leg of lamb
2 cloves garlic
1 tablespoon rosemary
  sprigs
2 teaspoons oil
freshly ground black
  pepper

1 Trim excess fat from lamb. Cut garlic cloves into thin slivers. Using a

Roast Leg of Lamb with Garlic and Rosemary

small sharp knife cut small slits over lamb and insert garlic and rosemary sprigs into slits.

2 Brush lamb with oil and sprinkle with black pepper. Place lamb on a rack over a baking dish. Add about ½ cup of water to baking dish.

Bake in a moderate oven (180°C), basting frequently with pan juice for about 1½ hours or until done as desired. Stand, keeping warm, for 10–15 minutes.

3 Serve lamb with Mint Sauce and seasonal vegetables.

HINT

Fresh rosemary is best for this recipe. If using dried rosemary chop finely and rub into the slits in the lamb.

23

PORK

Hand of Pork with Apricots

*M*odern methods of breeding and cutting pork have led to an increase in its popularity; new fashioned pork is much leaner, making it exceptionally tender, easily digestible and much healthier.

This leaner low-fat pork does not need a long cooking time, which makes meat stringy and dry. To calculate cooking time weigh meat; tie it into a compact shape if necessary for even cooking and roast in a moderate oven for 30 minutes per 500 g, plus an extra 30 minutes. For larger pieces of pork with their skin on, an initial 30 minutes cooking in a hot oven crisps the crackling.

Suitable cuts for roasting include leg, loin, shoulder, hand, rib on the bone and fillet.

Ask your butcher to remove rind from pork and to score the rind for crackling. Brush the cut surface with oil and a little salt or lemon juice. Roast in a hot oven with the rind uppermost until crisp and golden; pour off excess fat from rind during roasting. Traditional accompaniments to roast pork are Apple Sauce and Cranberry Sauce, served warm. Baked or fried apple slices may also be served.

2 Combine all ingredients for marinade. Cut deep slashes in the pork with a sharp knife, place in a baking dish and pour over marinade. Marinate in the refrigerator for at least 24 hours, basting frequently.
3 Drain off all except 2 tablespoons of marinade. Reserve. Bake pork in a moderate oven (180°) for 2½ hours. Baste frequently with reserved marinade.
4 Allow meat to rest for 15 minutes before carving. Serve with rice and salad. The remaining marinade may be heated and served as a sauce.

Hand of Pork with Apricots

Preparation time:
30 minutes plus 24
hours marinating
Cooking time: 2½ hours
Serves 8

¼ teaspoon mixed herbs
freshly ground black
pepper

1 hand pork weighing
2.5 kg
Marinade
1 x 425 mL can apricot
nectar
¼ cup white wine
2 tablespoons olive oil
2 cloves garlic, crushed
2–3 teaspoons curry
powder
1–2 teaspoons curry
paste

1 Remove rind from hand of pork to within 5 cm of knuckle by running your thumb around the edge of the hand just under the rind. Begin pulling from the widest edge, using your fingers to remove it from the fat. Cut through the rind at the knuckle with a knife.

Roast Pork Fillet with Apple and Mustard Sauce

Preparation time:
  30 minutes
Cooking time:
  35 minutes
Serves 4

750 g pork fillet
30 g butter
1 tablespoon oil
½ cup water
1 clove garlic, crushed
½ teaspoon grated fresh
  ginger
1 tablespoon seeded
  mustard
¼ cup apple purée
2 tablespoons chicken
  stock
½ cup cream
1 teaspoon cornflour

1 Trim the pork fillet, removing any fat or sinew from the outside. Tie the fillet with string at 3 cm intervals to keep a good shape.
2 Heat butter and oil in frying pan, add the pork fillet and cook until lightly browned all over. Remove and place pork on a rack in a baking dish. (Retain the cooking oils in pan.) Add water to baking dish and bake in a moderate oven (180°) for 30–35 minutes. Allow to rest for 10 minutes before slicing; keep warm.

3 To prepare Sauce: reheat remaining oils in pan. Add garlic and ginger, cook, stirring for 1 minute. Stir in mustard, apple purée and stock. Slowly stir in combined cream and cornflour and stir constantly until mixture boils and thickens. To serve pork, slice and spoon sauce over. Serve with roast potatoes and steamed broccoli.

HINT
Pork fillet is the section of meat that runs under the middle loin. Fillets can be thick fat fillets or long skinny pieces, and cooking time can vary because of this. To test for doneness use the pinch test.

Roast Pork Fillet with Apple and Mustard Sauce

Boned Pork Loin with Maple Glaze

Preparation time:
  30 minutes
Cooking time: 2 hours
Serves 8

1 x 2 kg piece boned
  pork loin, skin
  removed
30 g butter
2 tablespoons finely
  chopped chives
2 teaspoons ground
  coriander
½ teaspoon ground
  black pepper
⅓ cup maple syrup
⅓ cup brown sugar
30 g butter, melted
1 tablespoon seeded
  mustard

1 Remove excess fat from loin, leaving just enough to keep pork moist during cooking. Open loin out, spread with butter and sprinkle with chives. Roll up loin and secure with string, tying neatly at intervals. Sprinkle evenly with combined coriander and pepper.

2 Combine maple syrup, brown sugar, butter and mustard. Place pork in a baking dish on a rack. Brush with 1 tablespoon of maple syrup mixture. Pour some water into baking dish.

3 Bake pork in a moderate oven (180°) 1½ to 2 hours, basting frequently with maple glaze and adding more water to baking dish to prevent cooking juices and glaze from burning. When cooked cover with foil. Allow to stand 15 minutes before carving; keep warm.

4 Brush pork loin with remaining glaze, slice and serve with Piquant Plum Sauce (page 62) and roast vegetables.

Boned Pork Loin with Maple Glaze

HINT
Pork skin may also be rubbed generously with lemon juice, scored and grilled under a hot grill to give crispy crackling.

and Piquant Plum Sauce

1 Trim excess fat from pork and score at regular intervals. Rub combined spices evenly over pork.
2 Place onions over base of baking dish, put pork on top of onions and pour oil over pork. Pour water into base of baking dish. Cover with foil and bake in a moderate oven (180°) 1¼ hours.
3 Remove foil, sprinkle pork with brown sugar and bake a further 15–20 minutes or until golden. Allow meat to rest for 15 minutes before carving. Keep warm. Serve pork with vegetables or salad.

HINT
When testing roast meat for doneness with a meat thermometer, insert thermometer in the thickest part of meat away from fat or bone as this can cause inaccurate temperature readings. To determine doneness, calculate weight and refer to thermometer guidelines for accurate results.

Spicy Leg of Pork

Preparation time:
  30 minutes
Cooking time: 1¾ hours
Serves 6

1.5 kg leg of pork, skin
  removed

2 teaspoons ground
  cumin
2 teaspoons ground
  cardamom
2 teaspoons ground
  ginger
3 large onions, sliced
1 tablespoon oil
½ cup water
2 tablespoons brown
  sugar

Boned Pork Loin with Apple and Prune Stuffing

Boned Pork Loin with Apple and Prune Stuffing

Preparation time:
40 minutes
Cooking time: 2¼ hours
Serves 8

1 Granny Smith apple,
   peeled, cored and
   chopped
⅓ cup chopped pitted
   prunes
2 tablespoons port
1 x 2 kg piece boned
   pork loin
Sauce
2 tablespoons port
60 g butter, cubed

1 Combine apple,
prunes and port in a
small bowl. Spread
stuffing over meaty side
of loin. Roll up. Secure
with skewers or string.
2 Score pork rind and
rub with salt. Place on a
rack in a baking dish.
Bake in a hot oven
(200°) for 10 to 15
minutes. Reduce heat to
moderate (180°). Bake
for a further 1½ to 2
hours.
3 When cooked, cover
with foil. Allow to stand
for 15 minutes before
carving; keep warm.
4 Drain off all except 2
tablespoons of juice
from pan. Heat on top
of the stove and add
port. Bring to the boil,
stirring constantly, until
liquid is reduced by half.

5 Whisk in butter one
piece at a time. Serve
pork with sauce and
roast vegetables.

HINT
'Scoring' is the
culinary term for
slashing meat or rind
at regular intervals
through to flesh to
reduce cooking time
and ensure even
cooking.

Roast Butterflied Pork

Preparation time:
50 minutes plus
   overnight marinating
Cooking time: 2 hours
Serves 6

2 kg leg of pork, skin
   removed
2 cloves garlic, crushed
6 whole cloves
2 bay leaves
sprigs of fresh thyme
¼ cup oil
¼ cup lemon juice
½ cup red wine

1 Using a sharp knife
start at the thick end of
the pork leg and cut
down and around pork
bone. Working
carefully, scrape away as
much meat from bone as
you can; remove bone.
Cut down through the
thickest part of the meat,
but not right to the
bottom, so that pork can
be opened out flat.
2 Make several slits 1 cm
deep all over pork. Fill
with crushed garlic and
cloves. Place pork in a
flat glass dish and add
bay leaves and thyme.
Pour over oil, lemon
juice and red wine, cover
and marinate overnight.
3 Remove pork from
marinade; reserve
marinade. Place pork on
a rack in a baking dish.
Bake in a moderately
slow oven 1½ to 2
hours, basting
frequently with reserved
marinade. Allow to
stand for 15 minutes
before carving. Serve
pork warm or cold,
sliced with Apple Sauce.

HINT
When buying pork
look for flesh that is
light pink with
creamy white fat: this
indicates a tender cut.

POULTRY AND GAME

Roast Chicken with Tarragon and Bacon

It is important to store and handle poultry correctly. Always rinse and dry fresh poultry with absorbent paper, refrigerate and use within two days. Always defrost frozen poultry in the refrigerator or microwave oven; never let poultry stand at room temperature to thaw.

Poultry is usually sold according to weight. For example, a No. 16 chicken is a 1.6 kg bird. Calculate cooking time at 25 minutes per 500 g.

Chicken and turkey lend themselves to fruit-filled stuffings, blended with garlic, spices, nuts and breadcrumbs. Use fresh herbs liberally: try fresh mint, parsley, coriander and tarragon. Marinades and glazes flavour and tenderise chicken. For a flavour variation when roasting chickens, place on a layer of carrot and celery sticks in the baking dish — this also makes a tasty gravy.

When roasting geese and ducks, prick the skin across the breast and thigh area with a fine skewer. This releases excess fat from the bird. Baste well during cooking to keep bird moist.

Quails should be roasted until just tender; overcooking produces tough dry meat. The more simply game birds are cooked the better.

Accompaniments for goose and duck should be simple — perhaps roast potatoes or potato casserole, a seasonal vegetable or green salad. Traditional sauces include apple sauce, cranberry sauce and bread sauce.

Roast Chicken with Tarragon and Bacon

Preparation time:
  30 minutes
Cooking time: 1½ hours
Serves 4

1 x 1.5 kg chicken
2 large sprigs fresh
  tarragon or rosemary
15 g butter, melted
3 rashers bacon, rind
  removed

1 tablespoon oil
½ cup chicken stock
2 teaspoons extra fresh
  tarragon

1 Remove any loose fat from chicken; thoroughly clean and dry chicken. Place tarragon sprigs and butter in cavity of prepared chicken.
2 Lay bacon rashers criss-cross over chicken breast. Secure bacon in several places with small skewers or toothpicks.
3 Place chicken in a baking dish on a rack and brush with oil. Bake in a moderate oven (180°) for about 1½ hours, basting frequently with stock. (Cover chicken with foil if necessary to prevent overbrowning of bacon.) Allow to rest for 15 minutes before carving; keep warm.
4 Add extra tarragon to pan juices and pour over chicken to serve.

Hint

To defrost frozen birds health authorities strongly recommend thawing in the refrigerator as poultry is particularly susceptible to bacterial growth at room temperature. Take the chicken out of the freezer but don't unwrap it, because the skin tends to dry and toughen when exposed to air. Thaw completely in the refrigerator; this can take up to 24 hours for a 1.5 kg bird.

Traditional Roast Chicken with Mushroom Sauce

Preparation time:
 40 minutes
Cooking time: 1 hour
Serves 4

1 x 1.2 kg chicken
Stuffing
*2 cups fresh
  breadcrumbs*
1 onion, finely chopped
*1 rasher rindless bacon,
  chopped*
*125 g mushrooms, finely
  chopped*
*1 stalk celery, finely
  chopped*
*1 tablespoon chopped
  fresh parsley*
*1 teaspoon dried mixed
  herbs*
*freshly ground black
  pepper*
1 egg, lightly beaten
Sauce
30 g butter
250 g mushrooms, sliced
4 shallots, chopped
30 g butter, extra
1 tablespoon plain flour
¼ cup dry white wine
1 tablespoon sherry
¾ cup cream
pinch white pepper

1 Remove any loose fat
from chicken.
Thoroughly clean and
dry chicken. Set aside.
2 To prepare Stuffing:
combine all ingredients
for stuffing in a large
bowl. Mix well with
hands. Press into cavity
of prepared chicken.
Join cavity together with
a skewer.
3 Place chicken in a
baking dish on a rack.
Bake in a moderate oven
(180°) for about 1 hour.
Allow to rest for 15
minutes before carving.
Keep warm.
4 To prepare Sauce: melt
butter in a pan. Cook
mushrooms and shallots
for 2 to 3 minutes and
then remove from pan.
5 Melt extra butter. Add
flour. Stir well. Cook 1
minute. Remove from
heat. Gradually blend in
wine, sherry, cream and
pepper.
6 Return to heat. Cook,
stirring constantly, until
the sauce boils and
thickens. Stir in the
mushroom mixture and
simmer for 3 minutes.
Serve chicken with
sauce, roast vegetables,
peas and beans.

HINT

Store cooked poultry
for no more than 2–3
days in the coldest
part of the
refrigerator. Remove
stuffing from birds
and store it
separately. Reheat
stuffing in a moderate
oven for 30 minutes.
Always refrigerate
broth or gravy in
separate containers.

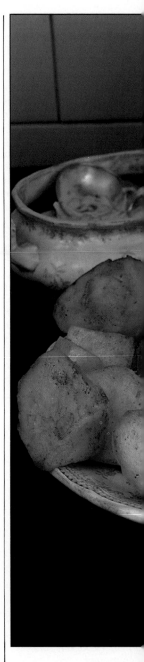

Traditional Roast Chicken with Mushroom Sauce

HOW TO STUFF AND TRUSS A CHICKEN

Place a knob of butter and a sprig of parsley in the body cavity. Loosely fill the chicken with stuffing, and truss. With a skewer, or large darning needle or trussing needle threaded with fine string, secure wings and flap over body cavity to enclose stuffing. Turn bird breast-side up and mould the stuffing into smooth even shape with the palms and fingers of both hands. Tie legs securely together with string and tie string around parson's nose, so that legs are neatly shaped to the bird.

Roast Chicken with Fruit Stuffing

Preparation time:
  40 minutes
Cooking time: 1½ hours
Serves 6

1 x 1.5 kg chicken
30 g butter
1 onion, finely chopped
½ cup chopped prunes
½ cup chopped dried
  apricots
½ cup seedless grapes
2 Granny Smith apples,
  peeled and sliced
½ teaspoon cinnamon
1 teaspoon brown sugar

*freshly ground black
  pepper*
30 g butter, extra
1 tablespoon lemon juice

1 Remove any loose fat from chicken. Thoroughly clean and dry chicken. Set aside.
2 Melt butter in pan, add onion and cook, stirring, until soft. Add prunes, apricots, grapes and apples and cook over a low heat for about 2 minutes. Stir in cinnamon and brown sugar. Spoon stuffing loosely into cavity of prepared chicken. Join cavity together with a skewer.
3 Rub extra butter over chicken and drizzle with lemon juice. Place chicken in a baking dish on a rack. Bake in a moderate oven (180°) for about 1½ hours. (Cover chicken with foil if necessary to prevent overbrowning.) Allow to rest for 15 minutes before carving. Keep warm. Serve chicken with pan juices and rice.

Roast Turkey with Cashew Nut Stuffing

Preparation time:
  50 minutes
Cooking time: 2–2½ hours
Serves 6–8

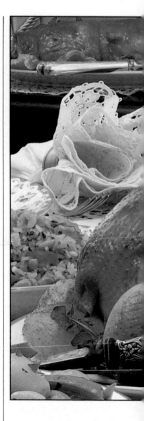

1 x 3 kg turkey
60 g butter
1 large onion, chopped
4 cups cooked brown
  rice
2 cups chopped dried
  apricots
1 cup unsalted cashew
  nuts
½ cup finely chopped
  parsley
⅓ cup finely chopped
  mint
2 tablespoons lemon
  juice
½ cup chicken stock
2 tablespoons oil

Roast Turkey with Cashew Nut Stuffing

Wine Gravy
¼ cup plain flour
1½ cups chicken stock
½ cup white wine

1 Remove neck and
giblets from inside
turkey. Wash turkey
well, dry with absorbent
paper and set aside.
2 Heat butter in pan,
add onion and cook,
stirring, until golden.
Combine butter and
onions with rice,
apricots, cashew nuts,
parsley, mint and lemon
juice; mix thoroughly.

3 Spoon stuffing loosely
into cavity of turkey.
Join cavity together with
skewer. Tuck wings
under turkey and tie legs
together. Place turkey on
a rack in a baking dish.
Bake in a moderate oven
for 2–2½ hours, basting
frequently with
combined chicken stock
and oil. Cover breast
and legs with foil after 1
hour so that skin does
not darken too much.
Allow to rest for 20
minutes before carving.
Keep warm. Serve with

roast vegetables and
wine gravy.
4 To make Wine Gravy:
drain off all except 2
tablespoons of fat from
baking dish. Place dish
over a low heat. Add
flour. Stir well to
incorporate all the
sediment. Cook, stirring
constantly, over medium
heat until well browned,
taking care not to burn.
Combine stock and
wine. Gradually stir into
flour mixture. Heat,
stirring constantly until
gravy boils and thickens.

37

HOW TO CARVE A TURKEY

A little practice and a sharp carving knife will soon have you carving confidently.

1 Cut into the bird where the ball joint of the wing meets the breast, and loosen the meat.

2 Continue cutting around the wing until the wing can be separated from the turkey body.

3 Tilt bird for a clear view of the angle of natural separation between the breast and thigh. Starting at the top, cut down through skin and meat to hip joint.

STEP-BY-STEP INSTRUCTIONS

4 Continue cutting through the hip socket until the thigh and leg section can be loosened and removed from the body. Place section on carving board.

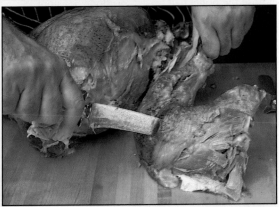

5 Separate thigh from leg by cutting through joint between. Cut meat from thigh into long, thin slices. Serve legs whole or sliced, according to size.

6 The breast is now ready to be carved. Start at the top of the breast, carving at an angle into thin slices.
Repeat all steps to carve remaining side.

Turkey Buffe with Apricot and Prune Stuffing

Preparation time:
  1½ hours
Cooking time: 2½ hours
Serves 8–10

1.5 kg turkey buffe
  (see Note)
Stuffing
3 cups fresh white
  breadcrumbs
1 cup chopped pitted
  prunes
1 cup chopped dried
  apricots
4 shallots, finely
  chopped
½ cup port
rind of 1 orange and
  1 lemon
1 egg, lightly beaten
Baste
1 cup apricot nectar
  (from canned apricots,
  see Garnish)
1 tablespoon brown
  sugar
2 tablespoons teriyaki
  sauce
Sauce
½ cup dried apricots
½ cup water
2 tablespoons brandy
1 chicken stock cube
1 cup water, extra
1 tablespoon cornflour
freshly ground black
  pepper
Garnish
Canned apricot halves
  in nectar (reserve
  nectar for basting)
Prunes

1 Defrost buffe in refrigerator (see Note).
2 To bone the buffe (see Note below and the Step-by-step instructions overleaf): using a small knife, beginning at the narrow end, ease the meat away from the bone along each side. Follow the contours of the bones, scraping where necessary.
3 Cut around the joint of the wing and lengthwise towards the body of the bird to expose the bone. Cut through the ligaments at the joint. Remove the bone.
4 Continue easing flesh off the rib-cage on both sides until the backbone is exposed. Cut along backbone to free meat.
5 To prepare Stuffing: in a bowl combine breadcrumbs, prunes, apricots, shallots, port and orange and lemon rinds. Mix until well combined and stir in beaten egg. Use hands to bind mixture. Spread down centre of boned turkey. Roll up.
6 Using a heavy duty needle and cotton sew the join. Tuck in the skin at the neck end and finish off securely.
7 Place turkey on rack in a baking dish. Bake in a moderate oven (180°) for 2½–3 hours, basting frequently with the combined apricot

nectar, brown sugar and teriyaki sauce. (Cover with foil if necessary to prevent overbrowning.) Allow to rest for 20 minutes before carving. Cover and keep warm.
9 To make Apricot Sauce: combine apricots and water in pan and bring to boil. Reduce heat and simmer until tender. Process or blend apricots until smooth. Return to pan and add combined brandy, stock cube, water and cornflour. Stir until mixture boils and thickens. Season with freshly ground pepper.
8 To serve turkey, decorate with apricot halves and prunes and brush with remaining apricot nectar mixture. Serve turkey buffe sliced with Apricot Sauce.

Note: A turkey buffe is the breast of the turkey on the bone. They vary in size from 1.5 kg to 5.5 kg. Turkey buffes are usually sold frozen. Frozen poultry should only be thawed in the refrigerator – the time will depend on the size of the buffe, about 24–36 hours. Do not unwrap the turkey while defrosting. If you do not wish to bone the buffe, stuff the neck cavity and continue as directed.

Turkey Buffe with Apricot and Prune Stuffing

STEP-BY-STEP INSTRUCTIONS

Boning and Stuffing a Turkey Buffe

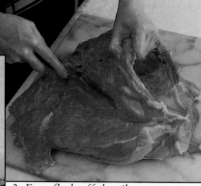

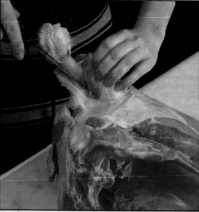

3. *Ease flesh off the ribcage.*

1. *Ease meat away from bone along each side, following contours of bones.*

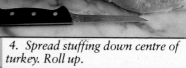

4. *Spread stuffing down centre of turkey. Roll up.*

2. *Cut around joint of the wing and lengthwise towards the body of the bird.*

5. *Sew up join. Tuck in skin at neck end.*

Oriental Chicken

Preparation time: 20
  minutes and overnight
  marinating
Cooking time: 1¼ hours
Serves 6

1 x 1.5 kg chicken
Marinade
¼ cup soy sauce
2 tablespoons teriyaki
  sauce
2 tablespoons honey
2 tablespoons dry sherry
2 tablespoons lemon
  juice
2 shallots, finely sliced
1 teaspoon grated ginger
¼ teaspoon five spice
  powder
¼ teaspoon sesame oil

Sauce
1 tablespoon cornflour
1 cup water
1 chicken stock cube

1 Thoroughly clean and
dry chicken. Place in a
plastic bag.
2 Mix together all
ingredients for marinade
in a bowl. Pour over
chicken. Seal bag. Place
on a plate. Marinate in
the refrigerator
overnight. Turn when
possible.
3 Remove chicken from
bag. Reserve marinade.
Place chicken in a baking
dish. Bake in a moderate
oven (180°) for 1¼ to
1½ hours. Baste
frequently with
marinade.

4 To prepare Sauce:
blend cornflour with a
little water. Combine
with remaining
marinade, water and
stock cube in a small
saucepan.
5 Heat, stirring
constantly, until sauce
boils and thickens.
Simmer for 3 minutes.
Serve chicken with
sauce, rice and salad.

HINT

To store unused fresh
ginger, peel, cut into
2 cm thick slices,
place in a screwtop
jar and cover with
sherry. Store in
refrigerator.

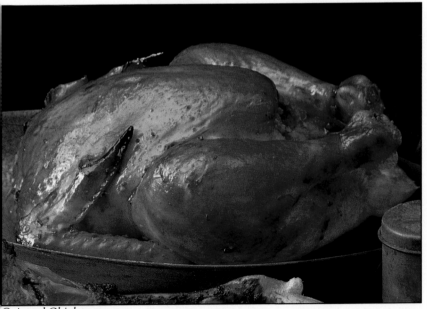

Oriental Chicken

HOW TO CARVE A DUCK

Follow these simple step-by-step instructions to cut and serve roast duck with skill and ease. You will need sharp poultry shears or kitchen scissors.

1 Rest bird for about 15 minutes after roasting. Starting at tail opening, cut with poultry shears through breast and up to neck.

2 Turn bird over and cut with shears on one side of the backbone and separate into halves.

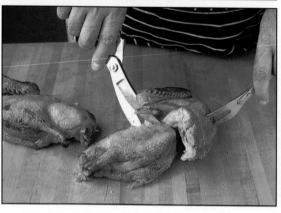

3 Follow the natural line between breast and thigh and cut crosswise into quarters. (Use this method to carve small game birds also.)

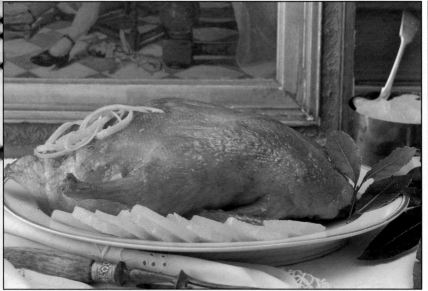

Duck with Orange Sauce

Duck with Orange Sauce

Preparation time:
  40 minutes
Cooking time: 1 hour
Serves 4

1 x 1.2 kg duckling
Stuffing
2 cups cooked rice
½ cup pine nuts
½ cup sultanas
4 shallots, chopped
juice and rind of 1
  orange
1 clove garlic, crushed
freshly ground black
  pepper
Sauce
2 tablespoons flour
1 cup white wine
½ cup orange juice
freshly ground pepper
2 oranges, segmented

1 Remove all loose fat from the duck. Wash and dry thoroughly. Set aside.
2 To prepare Stuffing: combine all ingredients for stuffing. Mix well. Press into the cavity of prepared duck. Join edges of cavity with a skewer.
3 Place on a rack in a baking dish. Bake in a moderate oven (180°) for about 1 hour. Remove from baking dish; keep warm.
4 To prepare Sauce: remove all except 2 tablespoons of juice from pan. Heat on top of stove. Add flour and stir well. Cook 1 minute. Stir in wine and orange juice off the heat.
5 Return to the heat. Cook, stirring constantly, until sauce boils and thickens. Simmer for 3 minutes. Blend in seasonings and orange segments.
6 Serve duck with sauce, potato casserole and vegetables.

HINT
If desired, rub a little salt into the skin of the duck for added crispness. Calculate cooking time for ducks at 20 minutes per 500 g.

Orange Garlic Duck

Preparation time:
 40 minutes
Cooking time: 1 hour
Serves 4

1 x 1.2 kg duckling
1 orange
6 cloves garlic, crushed
30 g butter
freshly ground black
 pepper
2 teaspoons plain flour
¾ cup dry white wine

1 Remove all loose fat from the duck, wash and dry thoroughly. Set aside.

2 Quarter orange. Combine garlic, butter and pepper; mix well. Put garlic butter into cavity of duck and add quartered orange. Join edges of cavity with skewer.

3 Place on a rack in a baking dish. Bake in a moderate oven (180°) for about 1 hour, basting frequently with pan juices. Remove from baking dish. Allow to rest for 15 minutes before carving; keep warm.

4 Drain all but 1

Orange Garlic Duck

tablespoon of fat from baking dish. Place baking dish over a low heat. Add flour. Stir well to incorporate all the sediment. Cook, stirring constantly, over medium heat until well browned, taking care not to burn. Gradually stir in wine and any juices from duck. Heat, stirring constantly until sauce boils and thickens. Serve duck with roast potatoes, onions and capsicums.

> **HINT**
> Before cooking a whole duck remove all the excess fat and press the oil glands near the base of the tail to empty them.

Roast Goose

Preparation time:
  40 minutes
Cooking time: 2½ *hours*
Serves 6

1 x 3 kg goose
30 g butter
1 onion, finely chopped
2 green apples, peeled
  and chopped
1½ cups chopped pitted
  prunes

3 cups small cubes of
  bread
2 teaspoons grated
  lemon rind
½ cup chopped parsley
1 tablespoon plain flour
1 tablespoon plain flour,
  extra
2 tablespoons brandy
1½ cups chicken stock

1 Remove all loose fat from goose. Using a fine skewer, prick the skin across the breast area. Set aside.
2 Melt butter in pan, add onion and cook, stirring, until golden. Combine butter and onion with apples, prunes, bread, lemon and parsley; mix thoroughly. Spoon stuffing loosely into cavity of goose, then join edges of cavity with skewer. Tie legs together.
3 Sprinkle a tablespoon of flour over goose. Place goose on a rack in a baking dish and bake in a hot oven (200°) for 15 minutes. Remove and discard any fat from baking dish. Prick skin of goose to remove excess fat. Cover with foil. Return to a moderate oven (180°) and bake for 2 hours, basting occasionally. Discard fat as it accumulates in baking dish. Remove foil, bake a further 15 minutes or until goose is golden. Remove from baking

dish. Stand 15 minutes before carving; keep warm.
4 Drain all but 2 teaspoons of fat from baking dish and place over a low heat. Add extra flour and stir well to incorporate all the sediment. Cook, stirring constantly, over medium heat until well browned, taking care not to burn. Gradually stir in brandy and stock. Heat, stirring constantly, until sauce boils and thickens. Serve goose with gravy, roast potatoes and creamed onions.

> **HINT**
> During roasting time, baste goose with its own, plentiful fat. This melts out more fat and helps crisp the skin.

Roast Quails with Bacon and Rosemary

Roast Quails with Bacon and Rosemary

Preparation time:
  40 minutes
Cooking time:
  25 minutes
Serves 4

8 quails
1 medium onion,
  chopped
3 rashers bacon,
  chopped
1 tablespoon fresh
  rosemary leaves
30 g butter, melted
½ cup port
¼ cup water
½ cup cream
1 teaspoon cornflour

1 Thoroughly clean and dry quails. Tie the legs and wings of each bird close to its body with string.
2 Spread onion, bacon and rosemary over base of baking dish and add quails. Brush each quail with melted butter. Pour ½ cup of combined port and water over quails.
3 Bake in a moderate oven (180°) for about 25 minutes. Allow to rest for 10 minutes before serving; keep warm.
4 Carefully strain any juices from baking dish into a small pan, add remaining port and water mixture and bring to the boil. Reduce heat and gradually stir in combined cream and cornflour, stirring until slightly thickened. Serve quail with sauce and roast vegetables.

HINT
When eating quail it is quite correct to use fingers after eating the flesh from the breast with a knife and fork. Provide guests with finger bowls filled with warm water; add lemon slices or fragrant flowers for a special touch.

HINT
Trussing keeps the bird in compact shape, ensures even browning and cooking and makes handling the bird easier.

VEGETABLE ACCOMPANIMENTS

Parsnip and Zucchini with Ginger and Almonds   *Glazed Carrots*

*F*resh seasonal vegetables make a perfect
accompaniment to roast meats.

Vegetables should be prepared as simply as
possible, cooked until just tender, dressed with
herbs and seasoned lightly. Serve two or three fresh
vegetables with roast meats to enhance and
supplement the roast.

In this chapter we share with you our secret for
the best roast potatoes, golden brown and crispy
outside, moist and soft inside. We've also included
favourites such as Sweet Nugget Pumpkins
Julienne, Braised Onions in Cream and Broccoli
with Browned Nut Butter Sauce.

Parsnip and Zucchini with Ginger and Almonds

Preparation time:
  15 minutes
Cooking time:
  10 minutes
Serves 6

3 parsnips, peeled and
  sliced
3 zucchini, sliced
1 teaspoon finely
  chopped fresh ginger
15 g butter
2 tablespoons toasted
  slivered almonds

Boil, steam or
microwave parsnips and
zucchini until tender.
Add ginger, butter and
toasted almonds; toss to
combine. Serve
immediately.

Glazed Carrots

Preparation time:
  15 minutes
Cooking time:
  15 minutes
Serves 6

8 medium carrots,
  peeled and sliced
60 g butter, melted
2 tablespoons brown
  sugar
1 tablespoon honey
chopped chives

1 Boil, steam or
microwave carrots until
tender.
2 Pour over combined
butter, brown sugar and
honey. Serve
immediately garnished
with chopped chives.

Braised Onions in Cream

Preparation time:
  20 minutes
Cooking time:
  25 minutes
Serves 6

18 tiny white onions,
  peeled and trimmed
300 mL cream
ground pepper

1 Place onions snugly in
a single layer in shallow
ovenproof dish.
2 In saucepan, heat
cream until simmering;
pour over onions.
Season to taste with
pepper.
3 Cover and bake in a
moderate oven (180°)
for 15 minutes. Remove
cover; continue baking
until onions are tender,
about 5–10 minutes
more.

HINT
Use sweet pickling
onions for this recipe.
For ease of peeling
top and tail onions,
taking care to keep
ends intact so that
onions do not fall
apart. Cover with
boiling water for
about 5 minutes to
loosen their skins,
drain and peel
immediately.

Left: Baby Vegetables with Herbs

Baby Vegetables with Herbs

Preparation time:
  15 minutes
Cooking time:
  10 minutes
Serves 6–8

1 kg seasonal baby
  vegetables
2 onions, chopped
60 g butter
¼ cup chopped parsley
¼ cup chopped fresh
  oregano or thyme
(or 2 teaspoons dried)
ground pepper

1 Trim vegetables and wash. If large, cut into even-sized pieces.
2 In large saucepan, cook onions in butter over moderate heat for 1 minute. Add vegetables and toss well to coat.
3 Cover vegetables; reduce heat and steam until all vegetables are crisp-tender, about 10 minutes.
4 Add parsley, herbs and pepper to taste.
Note. Choose from baby eggplant, carrots, baby squash (yellow or green), tiny onions, small green beans and zucchini; if using snow peas, add these near the end of Step 3 to avoid over-cooking.

HINT
When choosing vegetables, always demand freshness. Buying in season you get the freshest vegetables at the best price. Do not buy vegetables in sealed plastic-wrapped packs because they will sweat and spoil. Buy only what you need or can store without waste.

Right: Sweet Nugget Pumpkins Julienne

Sweet Nugget Pumpkins Julienne

Preparation time:
 30 minutes
Cooking time:
 45 minutes
Serves 8

4 *small golden nugget*
 pumpkins
30 g *butter*
freshly ground black
 pepper
4 *medium carrots*
300 g *orange sweet*
 potatoes
⅔ *cup water*
2 *tablespoons honey*
chopped parsley

1 Halve pumpkins and scoop out seeds. Place, cut side up, in baking dish. Dot each with ½ teaspoon of the butter; sprinkle with pepper.
2 Bake in a moderate oven (180°) until pumpkins are tender, about 45 minutes. Drain excess juice from halves.
3 When pumpkins are almost cooked, peel and cut carrots and sweet potatoes into short julienne sticks. Place in a saucepan with the water and honey.
4 Cover and heat until boiling; reduce heat and gently simmer until tender about 8 to 10 minutes. Drain well.

5 Spoon carrot and sweet potato sticks into pumpkins. Garnish with parsley.

HINT
If golden nugget pumpkins are not available substitute 1 whole medium-sized butternut pumpkin, scoop out seeds and flesh leaving a 2.5 cm pumpkin shell. Cook as directed.

53

Roast Potatoes

Preparation time:
  15 minutes
Cooking time: 1½ hours
Serves 6

8 *medium-sized Pontiac*
  potatoes, peeled
125 *g beef dripping or*
  lard or 125 mL oil

1 Cut any large potatoes
in half. Wash and dry.
2 Melt the beef dripping
in the roasting pan in the
oven. Add the potatoes.
Turn them in the fat to
ensure they are
thoroughly coated.
Roast in the upper half
of the oven, in a
moderate oven (180°),
for 30 minutes, turning
once.
3 Drain off all the fat
from the potatoes.
Continue to roast for 1
hour, turning once or
twice, until cooked,
crisp and golden.

HINTS

☐ Roast potatoes are
always crisper and
more golden if
cooked in a separate
metal roasting pan.
☐ For quicker
cooking, parboil
potatoes for 10
minutes, draining
well, before adding to
the fat.

Roast Potatoes, Capsicums and Onions

Preparation time:
  30 minutes
Cooking time:
  45 minutes
Serves 6

6 *medium-sized*
  potatoes, peeled and
  quartered lengthwise
1 *large red capsicum,*
  seeded and cut into 8
  wedges
1 *large green capsicum,*
  seeded and cut into 8
  wedges
4 *onions, quartered*
  lengthwise
4 *cloves garlic, finely*
  chopped
3 *tablespoons olive oil*
1 *teaspoon dried*
  rosemary
freshly ground black
  pepper

1 Arrange potatoes and
capsicum alternately in a
spoke pattern in a large,
shallow, ovenproof dish.
2 Pile onions in the
centre. Scatter garlic
over the top. Drizzle
with oil and sprinkle
with remaining
ingredients.
3 Bake in a hot oven
(200°) for 45 minutes or
until vegetables are
lightly golden, crisp and
tender.

Broccoli with Browned Nut Butter Sauce

Preparation time:
  10 minutes
Cooking time:
  15 minutes
Serves 6

Roast Potatoes, Capsicums and Onions

12 sprigs fresh broccoli
90 g butter
¼ cup slivered or flaked almonds
squeeze of lemon juice
freshly ground black pepper

1 Steam broccoli over simmering water, covered, until tender (about 8 minutes). Drain and arrange on heated serving platter; keep warm.
2 Meanwhile, in medium saucepan over moderate heat, melt butter. Add almonds and cook until both nuts and butter are browned. (Careful, don't let butter burn!)
3 Add a squeeze of lemon juice; pour over broccoli. Season to taste with pepper.

TRADITIONAL ACCOMPANIMENTS AND SAUCES

Apricot and Herb Stuffing

*T*hese traditional accompaniments are added extras that enhance roast meats. It certainly would be unfair on so splendid a dish as roast turkey to stint on sauces or stuffing and roast beef would not be half as grand without Yorkshire Pudding, a meaty gravy and horseradish sauce.

Accompaniments, sauces and stuffing help keep roast meats moist; they also provide contrasting colour, flavour and texture. Most importantly, they turn everyday meats into special occasion meals.

Apricot and Herb Stuffing

Preparation time:
  30 minutes
Cooking time: nil
Makes 3 cups

1 cup chopped dried
    apricots
¾ cup sultanas
1 onion, chopped
1 stalk celery, finely
    chopped
3 cups fresh
    breadcrumbs
1 tablespoon finely
    chopped parsley
¼ teaspoon dried sage
¼ teaspoon dried
    rosemary
¼ teaspoon dried thyme
1 egg, beaten

1 Mix all ingredients together in a large bowl. Place in a freezer container or plastic bag. Seal and freeze.
2 To use: thaw completely. Place in the cavity of the prepared turkey and seal cavity with a skewer. Roast turkey as directed.

Sage and Onion Stuffing

Preparation time:
  30 minutes
Cooking time: nil
Makes 3 cups

30 g butter
1 large onion, finely
    chopped
2 rashers bacon,
    chopped
1 tablespoon chopped
    fresh sage
2 teaspoons grated
    lemon rind
3 cups dry breadcrumbs
1 egg, lightly beaten

1 Heat butter in pan, add onion and bacon and cook, stirring, until soft. Combine onion and bacon with sage, lemon rind, breadcrumbs and egg. Mix thoroughly, seal and freeze until required.
2 To use: thaw completely. Place in the cavity of the prepared bird and seal cavity with a skewer. Roast goose as directed.

Walnut and Ham Stuffing

Preparation time:
  30 minutes
Cooking time: nil
Makes 3 cups

1 cup finely chopped
    ham
½ cup finely chopped
    walnuts
½ cup finely chopped
    mushrooms
2 cups fresh
    breadcrumbs
¼ cup chopped parsley
1 egg, lightly beaten

1 Mix all ingredients together in a large bowl. Place in a freezer container or plastic bag. Seal and freeze until required.
2 To use: thaw completely. Place in the cavity of the prepared bird and seal cavity with a skewer.

HINT
Butter a slice of day-old bread, rub with crushed garlic and place bread at the opening of the body cavity after stuffing a bird. The slice of bread acts as a lid and keeps stuffing from falling out.

1. Make a well in centre of sifted flour and salt; drop in eggs.

2. Stir in milk to make a smooth batter.

3. Carefully fill each muffin pan two-thirds full with batter.

Yorkshire Puddings

Preparation time: 15 minutes plus 1 hour standing
Cooking time: 20 minutes
Makes 8

1 cup plain flour
pinch salt
1 or 2 eggs
1 cup milk
1 tablespoon water
3 tablespoons lard or beef dripping, melted

1 Sift the flour and the salt together into a bowl. Make a well in the centre. Drop in the eggs. Gradually beat in sufficient milk to make a stiff but smooth batter, making sure there are no lumps. Gradually beat in the remaining milk. Strain into a jug. Cover and refrigerate for 1 hour. Stir in the water.
2 Spoon ¼ teaspoon of the fat into the base of each of 12 deep metal muffin pans. Place in a hot oven (200°) for 3 to 5 minutes to heat the fat. Carefully fill each muffin pan two-thirds full with batter.
3 Cook in a very hot oven (220°) for 15 to 20 minutes or until risen, golden and crisp. Serve at once.

HINTS
☐ The batter could be cooked in a 23 cm x 18 cm deep oblong metal tin.
☐ For a lighter batter, use skim milk or ⅔ cup milk and ⅓ cup iced water.
☐ 1 tablespoon of chopped fresh herbs or dried thyme to taste could be added to the batter for Herbed Yorkshire Puddings.

Yorkshire Pudding

Game Chips

Preparation time: 20
  minutes plus 1 hour
  standing
Cooking time:
  15 minutes
Serves 4

500 g old potatoes
oil for deep frying

1 Peel and slice potatoes
very thinly. Soak
potatoes in cold water
for 1 hour. Drain and
dry thoroughly on
absorbent paper.
2 Heat oil for deep
frying in a heavy-based
pan. Fry potatoes in
small batches until light
golden brown. Drain on
absorbent paper.
3 To serve, fry potatoes

again until crisp. Drain
and serve immediately
with roast turkey or
goose.

HINT
Substitute white
sweet potato for
potatoes for Game
Chips if desired.

59

Bread Sauce

Preparation time:
 15 minutes
Cooking time:
 25 minutes
Serves 4

1 small onion, finely
  chopped
1 cup milk
1 bay leaf
4 peppercorns
1 cup soft fresh white
  breadcrumbs
15 g butter

Place onion, milk, bay
leaf and peppercorns in a
small pan and simmer
for 20 minutes. Strain
and then stir in
breadcrumbs and butter.
Serve immediately.

HINT
Bread sauce is a
traditional
accompaniment to
roast turkey, goose or
chicken. Freshly
grated nutmeg and
ground cloves also
add flavour to this
traditional favourite.

Cumberland Sauce

Preparation time:
 15 minutes
Cooking time:
 10 minutes
Makes 2 cups

1 orange
1 lemon
1 cup redcurrant jelly
2 tablespoons French
  mustard
¼ cup port
freshly ground black
  pepper

1 Remove rind from
orange and lemon and
cut into fine strips.
Cover with water,
simmer over low heat fo[r]
5 minutes and drain.
2 Combine juice from
orange and lemon,
redcurrant jelly and
mustard in a small pan.
Heat gently, stirring
until jelly has melted.
Add port and simmer for
3 minutes.
3 Season with pepper
and add orange and
lemon rind to serve.

Back left: Bread Sauce, Right: Cumberland Sauce

Mint Sauce

Preparation time:
 10 minutes
Cooking time:
 10 minutes
Makes 1 cup

¼ cup water
¼ cup sugar

⅓ cup vinegar
¼ cup finely chopped
  mint

Combine water and sugar in small saucepan. Bring to the boil, stirring until sugar is dissolved. Add vinegar and bring to the boil again. Remove from heat and stir in mint. Cool. Stir well before serving. Serve with roast lamb.

HINT
Chop mint just before adding to vinegar to prevent discoloration.

Apple Sauce

Preparation time:
 20 minutes
Cooking time:
 30 minutes
Makes 2 cups

4 large green apples,
  peeled and cored
30 g butter
¼ cup white sugar
2 teaspoons grated
  lemon rind
¼ cup water

Place apples, butter, sugar, lemon rind and water in a heavy-based pan. Cook over a low heat, stirring frequently until the apples are soft and pulpy. Serve warm with roast pork, roast duck or goose.

HINT
Apple sauce may be made up to 3 days in advance and stored covered in the refrigerator.

Front left: Apple Sauce, Right: Mint Sauce

Piquant Plum Sauce

Preparation time:
  20 minutes
Cooking time:
  30 minutes
Makes 2 cups

1 *large onion, chopped*
2 *cloves garlic, crushed*
1 *tablespoon vegetable oil*
825 *g can dark plums, drained and pitted*
½ *cup water*

⅓ *cup lightly packed brown sugar*
2 *tablespoons white vinegar*
2 *teaspoons grated fresh ginger*
½ *teaspoon English mustard*
1 *small red chilli, finely chopped*

1 In large saucepan, cook onion and garlic in oil for 3 minutes. Add plums, water, brown sugar, vinegar, ginger, mustard and chilli; heat until boiling.

2 Reduce heat; simmer, uncovered, stirring occasionally, until plums are softened and sauce is thick, about 15 minutes. (If sauce becomes too thick, thin with a little water.) Serve hot with pork.

HINT
Use equal quantity fresh dark plums when they are in season.

Piquant Plum Sauce